Hard Work

A Day with Paramedics

By Jan Kottke

McGraw Hill SRA

Columbus, OH

From: A DAY WITH PARAMEDICS by Jan Kottke. Copyright © 2000 by Rosen Book Works, Inc.
Photo Credits: All photos by Thaddeus Harden
Contributing Editor: Jennifer Ceaser
Book Design: Michael DeLisio

SRAonline.com

McGraw Hill SRA

Printed in the U.S.A.

Send all inquiries to:
SRA/McGraw-Hill
4400 Easton Commons
Columbus, OH 43219-6188

ISBN 978-0-07-612271-4
MHID 0-07-612271-9

10 11 12 LHN 21

The McGraw·Hill Companies

Contents

My name is Tony.

This is my partner, Beatrice.

We are **paramedics.**

We help people who are sick or hurt.

859
NEW YORK PRESBYTERIAN
EMERGENCY MEDICAL SERVICES
5

We work in an **ambulance.**

We get a call on the radio.

A call means someone needs help.

EMERGENCY MEDICAL SERVICE

It's an **emergency!**

Someone is sick.

We drive fast to where the emergency is.

We are here!

We put the emergency **kit** on the **stretcher.**

We pull the stretcher out of the ambulance.

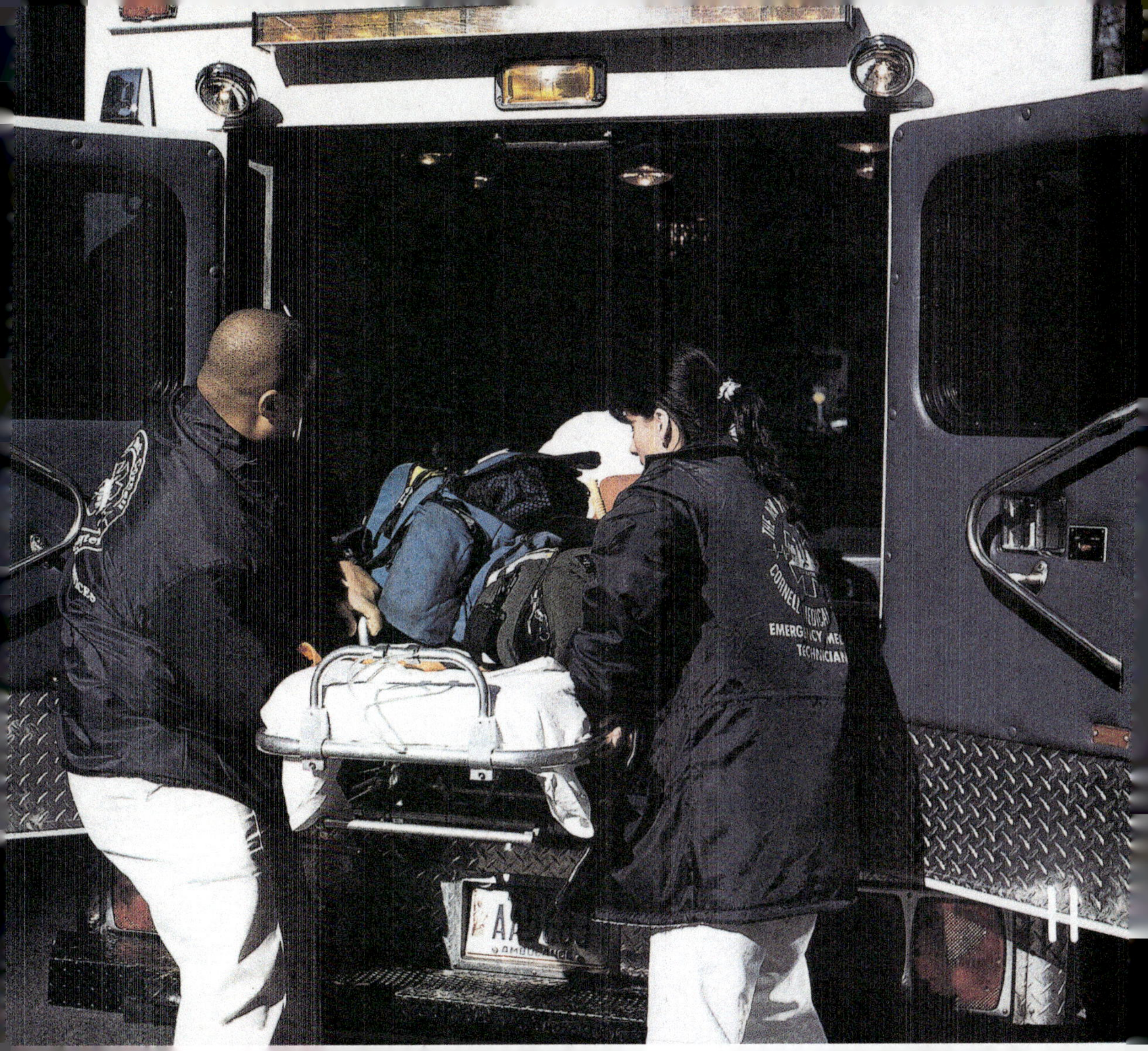

There's a woman who is sick!

Beatrice puts a **mask** on the woman.

It helps the woman to breathe.

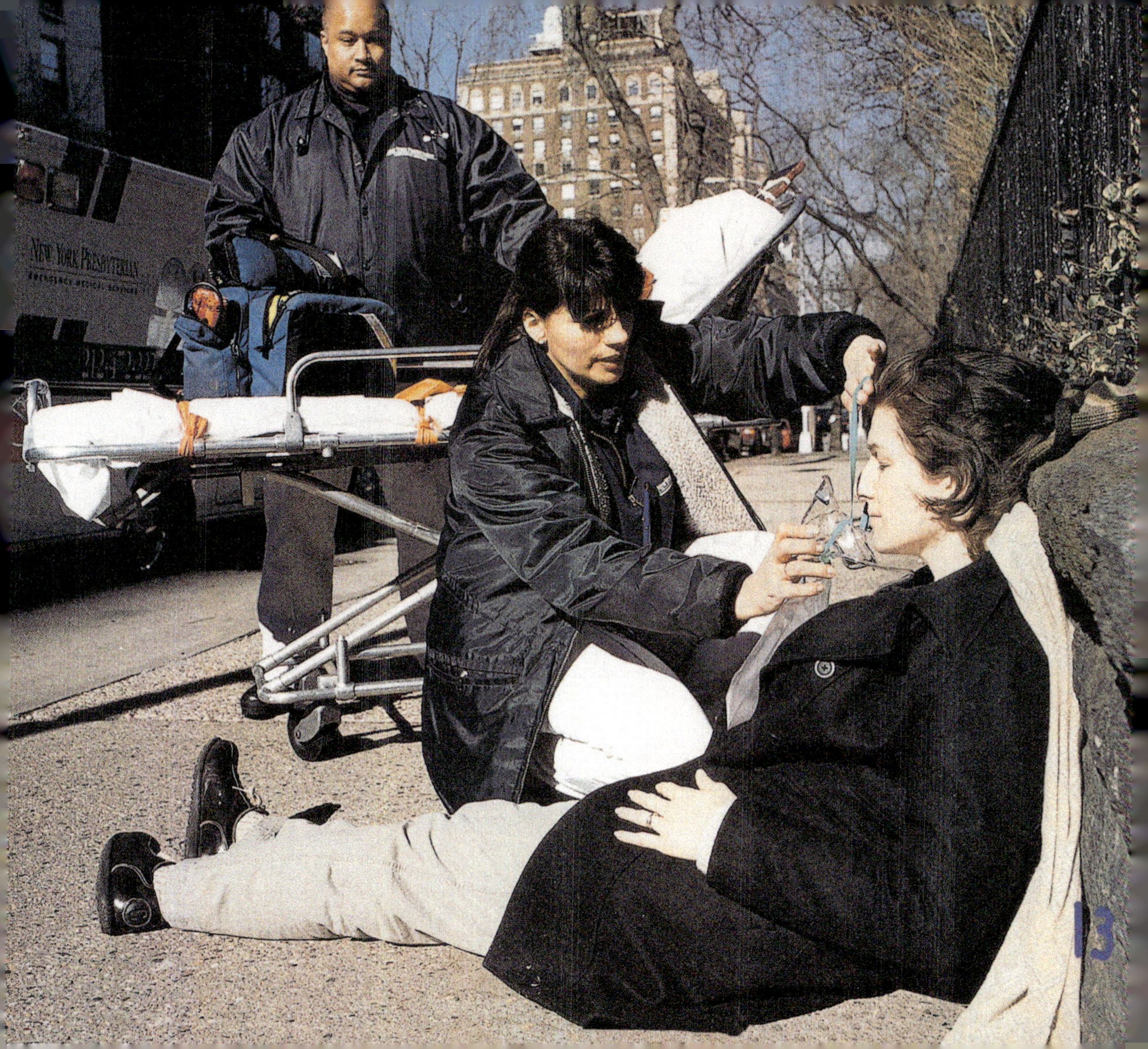
NEW YORK PRESBYTERIAN

We put the woman in the ambulance.

We will take her to the hospital.

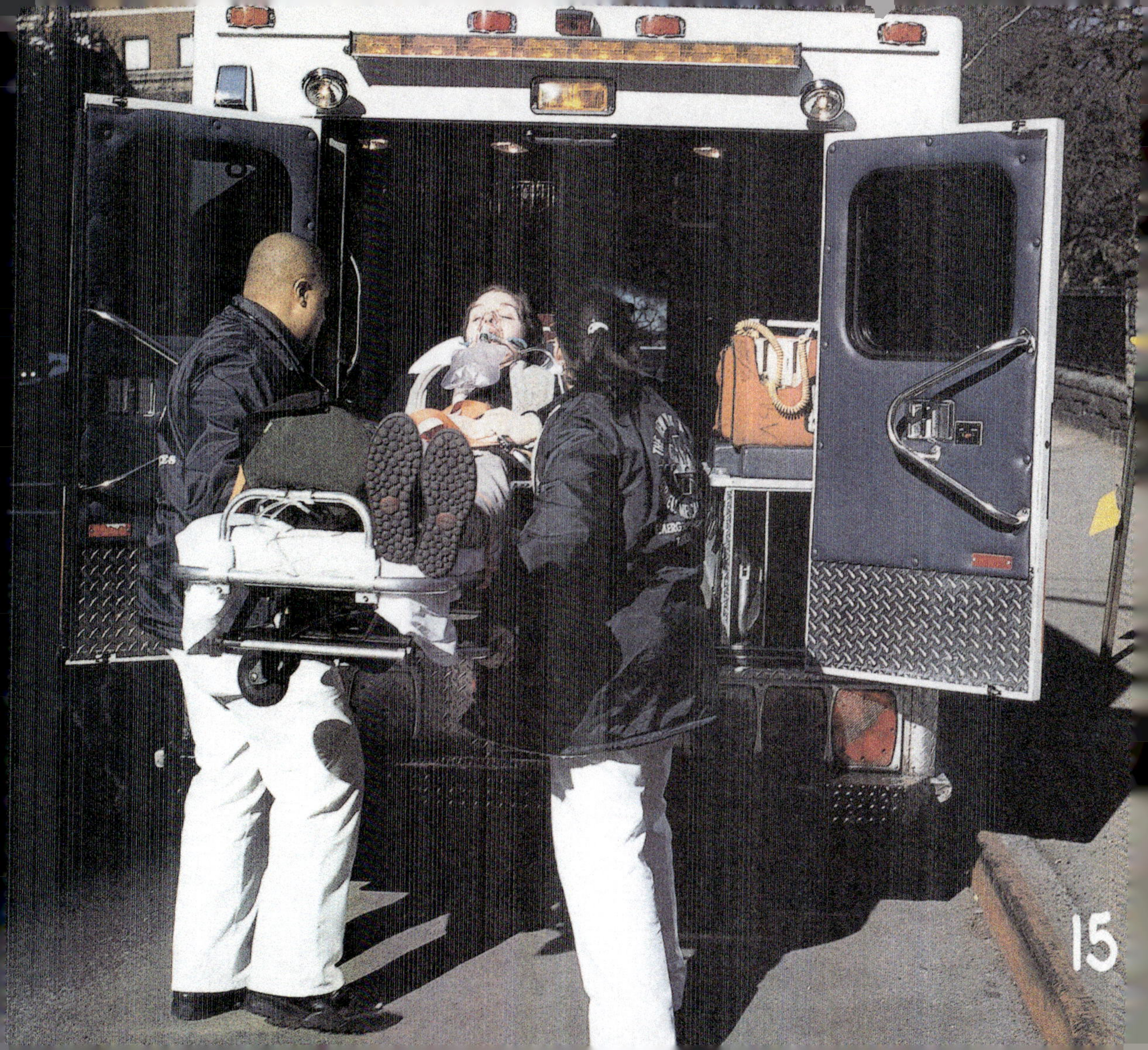

Beatrice stays in the back of the ambulance.

She **treats** the sick woman.

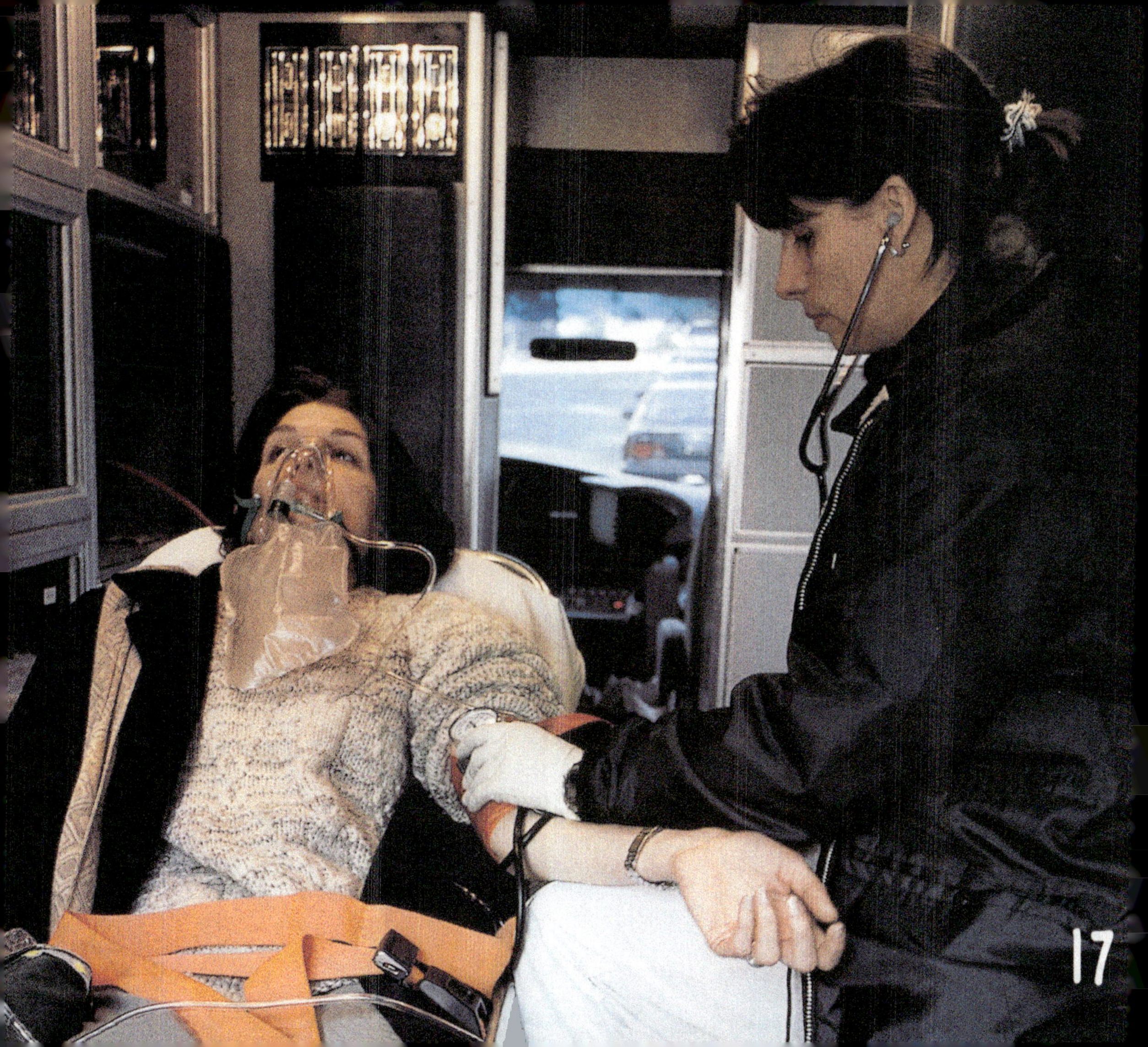

A doctor meets us at the hospital.

We tell the doctor what is wrong with the woman.

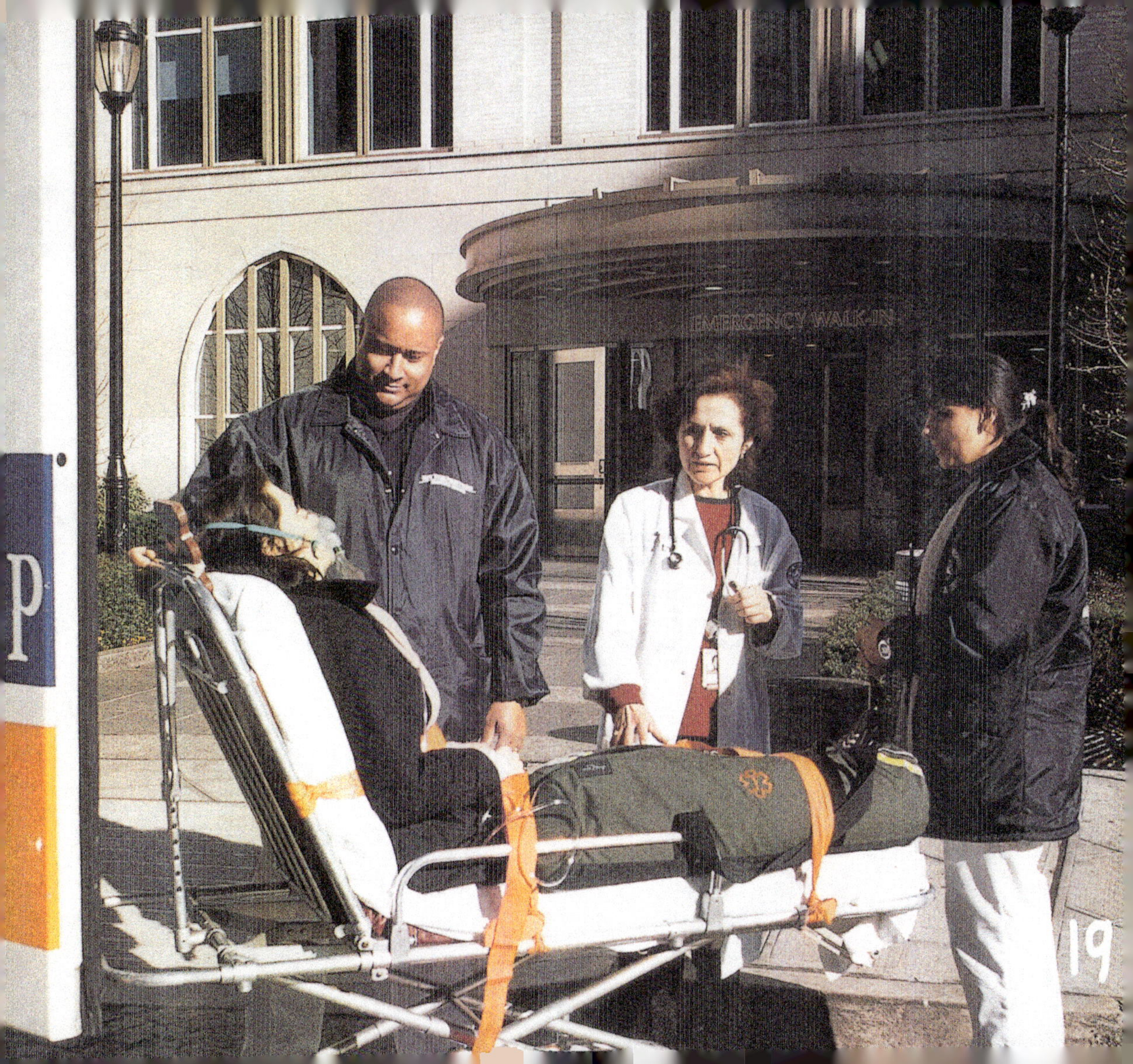
EMERGENCY WALK-IN
P

Our job is done.

Now we are ready for our next emergency.

859
NEW YORK STATE
CERTIFIED

New Words

ambulance (**am**-byu-lens) a truck that is used to take someone to the hospital

emergency (ee-**mir**-jen-see) a problem that needs attention right away

kit (**kit**) a bag of supplies used to treat someone

mask (**mask**) something that is put over a person's mouth and nose to help the person breathe.

paramedics (par -e-**med**-ix) workers who treat people at an emergency

stretcher (**strech**-er) a cot with wheels to move someone who is hurt or sick

treats (**treetz**) cares for someone who is sick or hurt

To Find Out More

Books

Ambulances
by Marcia S. Freeman
Capstone Press

Emergency!
by Gail Gibbons
Holiday House

Impatient Pamela Calls 9-1-1
by Mary B. Koski
Trellis Publishing

Web Site

The Kid Zone
http://firefighting.com/emtsue/kids
Print out and color emergency pictures. There also is lifesaving information and tips for using 911

Index

About the Author

Jan Kottke is the owner/director of several preschools in the Tidewater area of Virginia. A lifelong early education professional, she is completing a phonics reading series for preschoolers.

Reading Consultants

Kris Flynn, Coordinator, Small School District Literacy, The San Diego County Office of Education

Shelly Forys, Certified Reading Recovery Specialist, W.J. Zahnow Elementary School, Waterloo, IL

Peggy McNamara, Professor, Bank Street College of Education, Reading and Literacy Program